W9-CAH-760

PRESENTED TO:

BY

DATE

CLOSING
THE
GAP

OVER 40 WAYS TO GET FROM WHERE
YOU ARE TO WHERE YOU WANT TO BE

TODD DUNCAN

J. COUNTRYMAN
Nashville, Tennessee

TABLE OF CONTENTS

Section Four: Vocational Excellence

Section Five: Family Matters

Section Six: Personal Mastery

T he place is called Ant Island. In the opening scene of the popular Disney movie *A Bug's Life*, a group of ants is going about the task of collecting grain from nearby stalks. They regularly offer the grain to the grasshoppers, who in return, keep all other predators at bay, allowing the ants to live a full, rewarding, and safe life.

Here is how one scene unfolds: the ants are walking single file to the Offering Leaf when a shadow suddenly appears on the ground. One of the ants looks skyward and sees a leaf falling toward him. It lands and severs the line. The ant stops and panics, wondering how the line will continue. After some effort, Mr. Soil, one of the ant coaches, successfully moves the ants around the leaf, saying, "Here's the line again."

Princess Atta, the queen to be, realizes there is a gap and screams, "There's a gap! There's a gap! There's a gap in the line—what are we going to do?" Mr. Soil replies calmly by saying, "It's okay, your highness. Gaps happen! We just lost a few inches, that's all."

But Princess Atta continues to worry. She says to the queen mother, "What do we do now, Mother?" The queen, calm and collected, says, "We relax. We relax." And from that moment on, the ants are focused on *closing the gap*.

Here is the three-point message of this one minute of animation: first, gaps happen. They happen to us spiritually, financially, physically, vocationally, and in our relationships. Second, the distance between where we want to be and where we are often feels like miles, but with the right corrections it is, in fact, only inches. Third, focusing on another person's perspective, particularly someone who has dealt with similar issues, can often help us relax; only then can we learn what we must do to close the gap.

On the pages that follow, I have outlined forty-five gaps most of us will encounter at some point in our lives. Then, I have offered some practical ideas to help you close those gaps.

Balance in life is not a math problem; it is a design problem. It is not a willpower issue; it is a discipline issue. *Closing the Gap* is about discovering what is truly important and then designing a plan to deal with it.

I hope that you will be able to start closing whatever gaps you are experiencing in your life. My life's mission is to help you achieve the power to close as many gaps as possible so that you can live your life to the fullest. Let's go!

TODD DUNCAN

SUMMER 2000

God give me hills

to climb, and strength

for climbing.

ARTHUR GIUTERMAN

OPTIMUM
HEALTH

*Health alone
is victory.*

THOMAS CARLYLE

CHAPTER ONE

THE WEIGHT ISN'T WORTH IT

A recent issue of *Science* magazine found that 54 percent of American adults and 25 percent of American children are overweight. Other such studies report that as many as three in four Americans are too heavy! This is a problem that leads to all sorts of other health-related issues. If you are more than 20 percent above your optimum body weight, then it is time to close this gap.

You and I make choices each day about how we fuel the most important piece of equipment we own— our bodies.

Believe me, you can lose weight and can keep it off. Using the following steps, I lost forty-two pounds over twelve years ago and have kept it off to this day.

STEP 1: CHANGE THE MESSAGES YOU SEND TO YOUR BRAIN. Instead of sending a memo to your brain that says, "I'm fat," say, "I'm thin." Then immediately ask yourself, "What can I do this instant to give myself pleasure that doesn't involve food?" This shift in self-talk will help you change your eating habits.

STEP 2: TAKE INVENTORY. List the top one-to-five activities, relationships, and circumstances that typically zap your energy, get you down, or make you feel depressed or angry. What can you do to improve the way those situations make you feel?

STEP 3: SPEED UP YOUR METABOLISM. Most people do not realize that a faster metabolism is a basic requirement for permanent "thin gain" (instead of "weight loss"). Commit to thirty minutes of active stretching, weight lifting, or aerobic fitness at least every other day. This will raise your metabolism and increase your energy . . . and you will feel good about you.

CHAPTER TWO

THAT SECOND HELPING COULD KILL YOU

"I never eat more than I can lift!" boasts Miss Piggy, with a twinkle in her eye. Though we laugh at this delightful comment, many of us actually use it as a formula for life. Overeating, second helpings, and eating the wrong foods will make feel us sluggish, shorten our life span, and reduce our capacity to be who God designed us to be.

Guilt-driven diets produce only one result: failure. We lose every time. A well-executed *eating plan* is one of the most productive strategies for thinness available. Now is the time to work toward effective solutions in our eating habits.

The following four steps will help you develop an eating plan that works.

STEP 1: DECREASE THE PORTIONS; INCREASE THE NUMBER OF MEALS. A healthy plan generally involves five-to-seven meals a day. Obviously, these meals are smaller and more frequent. You should eat only one portion of each food—and each portion should fit into the palm of your hand. On this plan, you will eat less because you will be less hungry at each meal.

STEP 2: LOSE THE SUGAR. Recent reports indicate that adults consume, on average, twenty teaspoons of sugar a day, or 135 pounds of sugar per year. Most of us cannot metabolize the sugar we consume because sugar quickly turns to fat. Especially watch out for sodas, most desserts, and foods with "added sugar."

STEP 3: STOP EATING "FAT FREE." "Fat free" is a myth. Most people increase their portions when eating fat free, which results in eating too much of the wrong kind of fat. We *need* fat. However, we need more of the right kinds of fat— polyunsaturated and monounsaturated. But we should limit even our "good" fat intake to 20 to 30 percent of our daily calorie consumption.

STEP 4: DRINK SIXTY-FOUR OUNCES OF WATER A DAY. Water enhances metabolism and increases the "flushing" process of bad fats. When consumed before a meal, water also reduces hunger and food intake.

CHAPTER THREE

BUT IT'S SO BORING

G od gave us bodies that need physical activity, but too many of us are couch potatoes. We load ourselves down with so much fat and food that going to the gym, riding a bike, or even taking a walk around the block are the farthest things from our minds. The good news is that exercise can be fun. Here are some ways to help you close the exercise gap.

"God gave you your body! Life has a 100 percent mortality rate. Glorify God in your body and in your spirit, which are His." PARAPHRASE OF 1 CORINTHIANS 6:19–20

According to a July 1997 article in *USA Today*, over 60 percent of American adults are deficient in the "activity department." The statistics are alarming. Only 22 percent meet the minimum exercise guidelines of thirty minutes of moderate activity most days of the week. And yet, 97 percent already know that physical activity is good for them. The issue is motivation. The following four steps will help you begin your physical activity program today.

STEP 1: ADD THE FUN FACTOR. Make your workout fun. Listen to music or books on tape, read, or watch television.

STEP 2: ADD THE FRIEND FACTOR. The Bible says, "Two are better than one, because they have a good reward for their labor" (Eccles. 4:9). Exercising with a friend increases accountability and consistency.

STEP 3: ADD THE FUDGE FACTOR. Give yourself one or two days off each week—days without exercise that are free from worrying about food consumption. These fudge days makes the other days easier.

STEP 4: ADD THE "NOW" FACTOR. Whenever you think about exercising, do it immediately. If you give yourself too much time to think, then you will make excuses.

CHAPTER FOUR

TOO MUCH OF A BAD THING

My friend Hyrum Smith, CEO of the Franklin Covey Company, defines *addictive behavior* as "compulsive behavior with short-term benefits and long-term destruction." Addictions are a reflection of a lack of self-worth and a need for inner health. In virtually every case, addictions persist because we are trying to escape from low self-esteem. Lasting, healthy self-esteem, which gives us the power to conquer addictions, comes only when we measure our worth by God's unconditional love—not by our capacity to "get it right" by ourselves. One of the most common and damaging addictions is alcohol. Returning to a level of managed sobriety is not easy, and an addicted person will need help to overcome it. However, it is possible to close this ruinous gap.

King Solomon gives great advice for people who drink too much. Some three thousand years ago, he created a remarkably clear word-picture of alcohol: "Do not look on the wine when it is red, when it sparkles in the cup . . . at the last it bites like a serpent, and stings like a viper. Your eyes will see strange things, and your heart will utter perverse things" (Prov. 23:31–33).

I can remember clearly when I decided to change my drinking behavior: I had learned the statistics and then considered them in relation to my health. Studies have shown that one to two glasses of wine per day can decrease the risk of heart disease. However, moderation can lead to excess, and excess drinking can cause a stroke, high-blood pressure, heart disease, cancers, or cirrhosis of the liver—so why risk a premature death?

When you drink one or two glasses of wine per day, you also are adding a whopping sixty-two pounds of calories to your body each year. These sugar calories turn to fat easily. Other side effects include reduced mental clarity and energy.

Starting today, think of your body as God's temple, a masterpiece that He does not want you to ruin. Each day, God offers you new opportunities to live well. Begin to take advantage of them.

CHAPTER FIVE

GOING UP IN SMOKE

n the United States, current estimates say that 25.2 million men (26.7 percent) and 23.2 million women (22.8 percent) are smokers, which increases their risk of heart attack, lung cancer, osteoporosis, hearing loss, and stroke. Smokers also feel and look older.

In addition, 4.1 million teenagers, between the ages of twelve and eighteen, are already habitual smokers. Sadly, more than six thousand other teenagers try a cigarette each day, and more than three thousand of those same teenagers become regular smokers every day. If trends continue, approximately five million young people, children under eighteen years old, will die eventually from a smoking-attributable disease. Do these statistics convince you that it is time to close the gap?

Let me tell you a story. For many years, my parents smoked an average of three to four packs of cigarettes per day. But after my dad became a radiologist, he saw and brought home lung x-rays of patients who had died from smoking-related diseases. We saw healthy lungs become cloudy, congested by tar, nicotine, and cancer. During that time, my dad quit smoking, and I decided that I was never going to smoke.

Why do you smoke? Do you think you look cool? Do you feel alive with energy each time you light up?

Or do you have a sickening, phlegm-rich hack? Are your teeth and fingernails yellow?

Ask your doctor to show you some lung x-rays of dead people. Then, ask yourself, "Does smoking make sense to me?" If it doesn't, I encourage you to do the following.

STEP 1: Set the date that you will become a nonsmoker. Link a major reward to that day.

STEP 2: Commit to a daily plan that coincides with your target date in step one. For example, if you want to go from twenty cigarettes a day to none, lower your intake by just one per day by following a twenty-one day plan.

STEP 3: Ask a nonsmoking friend to hold you accountable while you are on your new plan.

CHAPTER SIX

I'M SICK!
WHY ME?

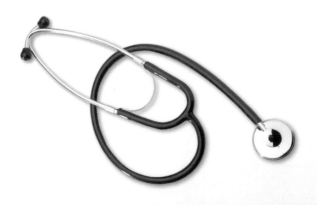

Sometimes we do everything right for our health, or so it seems, but we still become sick—sometimes very sick. We may suffer from severe allergies, a bad back that prevents us from playing with our children or grandchildren, chronic fatigue syndrome, failure to recover from a serious accident, or a terminal disease. This is when we need extraordinary help to get us through terrible times. This gap is very difficult to close. Fortunately, there are proven, effective ways to accept our health challenges, even with a joyful heart.

Two years ago, my friend Mary was diagnosed with breast cancer. In the days, weeks, and months that followed, she did five important things to combat her disease.

1. SHE GATHERED KNOWLEDGE. When a major illness threatens you, acquire as much knowledge as you can about it. Seek out other opinions.

2. SHE HAD AN UNQUENCHABLE POSITIVE ATTITUDE. Mary said, "I'm going to beat this thing!" and "I am not through living!" Research is now conclusive that the prognosis is better when the patient's attitude is positive.

3. SHE JOINED A SUPPORT GROUP. Hope still springs eternal. There is no better way to hold onto hope than to hang out with people who have been there—or who are *still* there.

4. SHE DID A FAITH CHECK. Get right with God if you haven't already. In Him you will find the strength to battle anything.

5. SHE PRAYED "WITHOUT CEASING" (1 Thess. 5:17). Mary prayed daily to be cured. Her friends, including me, also prayed with her on the phone and in person.

In the end, Mary survived. She is now helping a friend deal with the same illness. God is using Mary to make a difference in the lives of others. When you or someone you know is severely ill, do you simply *go* through it, or do you *grow* through it?

CHAPTER SEVEN

SOMEONE I LOVE IS ABOUT TO DIE

S aying good-bye to someone you love is one of the most difficult and traumatic times of our lives.

Whether it is a parent, grandparent, child, neighbor, former coach, pastor, or counselor, the death of someone dear is a sobering experience. When a loved one is about to leave us, we will invariably say to ourselves, "I wish I had spent more time with them . . . I wish I had told them *in life* how much I really loved and appreciated them." While it may be too late to reach out to someone who has already passed away, it is not too late to treat the loved ones who are still living with love and no regrets. With a few simple "love tools," you can begin to close this gap today.

The call from my wife was gut wrenching: "Honey, we have been in a terrible accident." Sheryl—who was pregnant with Matthew, our second son—and Jonathan, my son, were taken by ambulance to the hospital. Sheryl went to one emergency room, and Jonathan went to another. But I am happy to say the God gave me another chance to show my family how much I cherish them. To this day, I never leave home or hang up the phone without telling them how much I love and value them.

In less than one minute, John F. Kennedy Jr., his wife, and his sister-in-law plunged from the sky into the ocean off of Martha's Vineyard. Three days later, their bodies were found.

In the blink of an eye, life can change. Do the important people in your life know how much you care? Have you told them lately that you love them? Do you focus on them with the realization that they could be gone tomorrow? Tough questions? You bet.

Sometimes, we know in advance that our time with those we love is limited. In 1990, Sheryl's mom, Wilma, was diagnosed with Lymphoma, a disease she battled courageously for eight years. During that time, I watched Sheryl increase her communication with her mom. Sheryl created lasting moments by acknowledging important occasions and seizing every opportunity to let her mom know she loved her. When the cancer worsened and the time grew short, Sheryl flew back and forth to Michigan as many as two times a month to be with her mom. Wilma died two weeks before Thanksgiving in 1998. As she deals with the loss even today, Sheryl knows she gave her mom the feeling of unquestionable love while she was alive.

Add value. Make a difference. Although you cannot escape the pain and grief of loss, your conscience will rest easier if you showed them unselfish love while they were living.

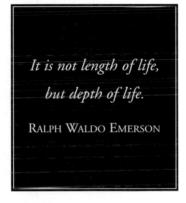

*It is not length of life,
but depth of life.*

RALPH WALDO EMERSON

MAXIMUM WEALTH

Make all you can,

Save all you can,

Give all you can.

JOHN WESLEY

CHAPTER EIGHT

TOMORROW? *WHAT* TOMORROW?

f you are looking for a comfortable nest egg for your later years, then there are certain economic principles you must apply today. One of the most important, and perhaps the most painful, is *delayed gratification*.

If you want something of greater value later in life, then you cannot put something else in its place today. Only by *paying now* will you be able to *play later*. To tinker with this formula is to invite disaster. If you are living with this equation reversed, then you are probably already in trouble, whether you know it or not. It's time to close the gratification gap.

What do you value more: things or money?
Which makes more sense to you: pay now and play later, or
play now and pay later? You need to make a choice. The following laws will help you develop discipline with your money.

LAW 1: TRACK YOUR CASH OUTFLOW. Until we
start tracking where our money goes, we will not know how
much we are spending or what we are buying.

LAW 2: UNDERSTAND THE COST OF WAITING.
Start saving today. Consider these facts from *Money* magazine:

Age when lifetime savings begins	Yearly contribution	Lifetime contribution	Lifetime Interest earned at 6%	Total savings
21	$5,000	$220,000	$832,029	$1,052,029
31	$5,000	$175,000	$365,918	$540,918
41	$5,000	$120,000	$140,397	$260,397

LAW 3: UNDERSTAND THE POWER OF COM-
POUNDING. The wealth-building mantra is *pay now, play
later, and invest the difference.* When money is left undisturbed
over time, it can actually outpace the amount of your current
contributions.

Save one penny per day. Every day, add another penny. Let
it compound daily for thirty days at 100 percent. At the end of
one month, you will have $5,368,710. Now you may ask, "Isn't
100 percent an unrealistic rate of return?" Yes! But here's one
for you, *Is one penny per day an unrealistic investment?*

CHAPTER NINE

THE SORRY STATE OF MY ESTATE

According to the Social Security Administration, if you randomly selected one hundred people and followed them from age twenty-five to age sixty-five, this is what you would find:

- 19 have died.

- 15 have incomes over $30,000.

- 66 have incomes less than $30,000.

Surprised? These statistics reflect the overall lack of knowledge that most people have about the average person's financial status. Because of this, they do not seek out and implement financial advice. Additionally, they have not created the proper wills, trusts, and estate planning documents to protect their estates from unnecessary and excessive taxes.

Have you sought out a trusted advisor who can help you with your financial future? If not, let's close this gap in your finances.

Three of the top five reasons people fail
financially are:

- They fail to create a financial plan.
- They make poor investment choices.
- They procrastinate in starting a savings plan.

There will come a day when you will not be able to work.
Therefore, it is paramount that you organize your finances
long before that time comes—and a trusted advisor can help.
Such advisors should be knowledgeable and should have a successful track record. They should also be interested in you and
should ask about your financial goals.

My brother Jeff is a top financial planner with Lincoln
Financial Advisors. He recommends the following checklist to
clients who want to prepare for their financial futures. If you
want to avoid becoming one of the many bleak statistics on
the financial battlefield, then consider these steps:

- During your twenties: Start a savings program, identify
your long-term financial goals, train for a career, determine
your life- and disability-insurance needs, protect your belong-
ings with automobile and personal property insurance, and
consider opening an IRA.

- During your thirties: Open an IRA, invest for capital
growth, write a will, and explore your retirement goals. If you
have children, buy more insurance to provide for a growing
family and expanding house needs, name a guardian for your
children, and begin to build an education fund.

- During your forties: Diversify your investments, develop an estate plan, seriously think about retirement planning, review and revise your will as necessary, explore a living will and power of attorney, re-evaluate your insurance policies (including homeowners, life, disability and umbrella liability), and consider deferred compensation plans with your employer.

- During your fifties: Evaluate and update your retirement plans, plan for long-term health care, invest so that your assets continue to grow as well as produce necessary income, decide where you want to live in the first part of your retirement, review your estate plan (including will, trusts, and liquidity of assets), and fulfill any responsibilities associated with aging parents.

- During your sixties: Re-evaluate your budget in relation to your retirement needs, reduce your taxable estate, shift a portion of your assets from growth to income producing, investigate part-time employment or volunteer work. Additionally, ensure long-term care needs are met, set up any additional health insurance you may need to supplement Medicare, review any will and trusts as well as life insurance. Lastly, if applicable, make any necessary plans for transitioning the family business.

- During your seventies: Shift most or all investments from growth to income, update your living will and power of attorney, share your financial decisions with other family members. If you have children, investigate gift and insurance plans for them and for any grandchildren, explore charitable giving plans, and negotiate shifting business interests, if applicable.

*The highest use of
capital is not to make
money, but to make
money do more for the
betterment of life.*

HENRY FORD

CHAPTER TEN

THERE'S NOTHING IN MY PIGGY BANK

On average, Americans save 5 percent of their disposable income. Japanese households are socking away 12.2 percent. The Germans are saving 11.5 percent, and thrifty Belgians are putting aside 17 percent, according to figures provided by the Organization for Economic Cooperation and Development.

We are not yet a nation of savers. The United States holds 14 percent of the world's total savings, yet we borrow 27 percent of the capital available in the world market. That's the big picture. What about you and your personal savings plan? It is time to close the gap.

Cash management is the secret to wealth building. We must spend less than we make. Most surveys show that people are spending their disposable incomes on things they do not need. The following steps will help you start your savings plan today.

STEP 1: ADJUST YOUR LIFESTYLE. Researchers Thomas Stanley and William Danko, authors of the *New York Times* best-selling book *The Millionaire Next Door*, have determined that the nation's wealthiest first-generation millionaires shared this commonality: *they lived well below their means.* Their rule: pay now; play later.

STEP 2. REDUCE YOUR DEBT. One of the killers of financial freedom is high-interest rate debt, the most common of which is credit card debt. Credit cards can destroy your net worth, and they can have a devastating impact on your self-worth. To close this gap, make this debt manageable, and pay it off gradually as you work on other financial goals.

STEP 3: DEVELOP AUTOMATIC CASH ALLOCATION. Set up automatic deductions from your paycheck for investment purposes. This is very common with mutual funds, for example. Your check will be less, but your money will now be working for you.

Once you have set these steps in motion, you will be on your way to filling your piggy bank.

CHAPTER ELEVEN

THIS "INVESTMENT" LOOKS GOOD TO ME

Most people—young, old, and every age in between—have a burning desire to be better off financially. This desire makes us easy prey for financial scams and risky investments.

Statistics state that sixty million Americans get suckered into some kind of scam every year. How much do we lose? About $200 billion. The two largest scams are related to personal finance and health. They promise enough money to "enjoy the good life." However, the quick-and-easy money, the big amounts, and the enormous guarantees never really pan out.

Smart investors do not take the bait. They follow the rules of sound investing and avoid get-rich-quick products. If you have ever looked for the quick buck and found yourself victimized by such schemes, then it is time to close the gap!

You've worked hard to earn your money. Shouldn't you work equally hard to keep it? The Bible offers good advice on this topic: "He who has a slack hand becomes poor, but the hand of the diligent makes rich" (Prov. 10:4). Essentially, nothing worthwhile and lasting comes easy.

Here are three rules to help you avoid risky investments:

RULE 1: FAST EQUALS SLOW. Chances are, if you are broke, it is not because of what happened today, but rather what didn't happen in the weeks, months, and years past. Most people's monetary challenges come from long-term abuse of the financial rules.

RULE 2: NEVER REVEAL YOUR CREDIT CARD NUMBER. Professional scam artists try to obtain your credit card number by selling something to you or by claiming they need it to verify who you are. They may pose as a bank representative or someone with a "hot investment."

RULE 3: REMOVE THE EMOTION. Do not buy anything when your emotions are high. We make our poorest financial decisions when we feel the peak emotion of a potential payoff. For example, when no one has won the lottery for several weeks, the intensity of emotion becomes very strong. As a result, some people will spend $200 for tickets, instead of their usual weekly allocation of $10—even though their odds of winning are still almost zero!

CHAPTER TWELVE

MINIMUM PAYMENT—
MAXIMUM PAIN!

C onsumer credit in the United States has reached the unprecedented level of $1.23 trillion. Credit card debt alone amounts to $528 billion of that total. How much of that debt is yours? Roughly two-thirds of Americans who have credit cards do not pay off their monthly balance. If you are making minimum payments on your credit card balances, then you are going through maximum pain—whether you realize it or not. It is time for you to close the credit card gap.

For most Americans, one of the biggest challenges to building wealth is debt. Credit cards and department store charge cards carry the highest interest rates among all types of consumer credit. Since most of this debt is accumulated over time, it often seems insurmountable when the task of paying it off hits home.

If you are weary of your balances never going down, and if you are abusive with this type of high-cost lending, your first mental shift must be long-term. You must first manage how the debt is being created before you can ever begin to reduce the overall amount of the debt. Here are five keys to escaping the credit card jungle:

KEY 1: MAKE A LIST. List all credit cards, department store cards, and personal loan creditors, along with balances owed and the interest rates. Put the highest rate on the top of your list.

KEY 2: PICK YOUR NUMBER. Decide the maximum dollar amount you can "pledge" toward reducing debt on a monthly basis. Stretch. Most people can adjust their lifestyle on a short-term basis to produce between $100 and $200 a month in freed-up cash.

KEY 3: ACCELERATE YOUR PAYMENTS. On all cards, except your highest, pay the minimum balance plus an extra 5 to 10 percent. Allocate whatever is left over to your highest interest-rate card; this amount should be much higher than the total "extra" you paid toward the other cards. The goal: Pay off the highest interest-rate card first and then repeat the process on the next highest interest-rate card.

Here's what would happen if you paid the minimum, or more, every month on a $2,705 balance, with an interest rate of 18.38 percent:

Payment Rate	Time to Pay Off	Interest Paid
2% of balance	27 years, 2 months	$11,047.00
4% of balance	8 years, 5 months	$2,707.00
8% of balance	2 years, 1 month	$94.00

KEY 4: SWITCH TO A CASH MENTALITY. Here is how it works. Use only one low-interest, no annual fee (preferably) credit card. Decide on its preset limit, and *charge nothing unless you have the cash equivalent to pay for it now*—unless, of course, it is an emergency. Important: Do not carry the card with you.

KEY 5: ALTERNATIVE OPTIONS. You have two other options that may also help. The first is balance transfer—that is, move debt from one high interest-rate card to a lower interest-rate card. When the transfer is done, call the creditor on the higher-rate card and close the account. The second option utilizes an equity line of credit. In addition to the benefit of a much lower interest rate, typically prime plus three, the interest is tax deductible. Do not take out an equity line without having your high-interest rate accounts closed.

If you have come this far, you are on your way to closing this miserable, self-defeating gap.

*The greatest
wealth is to live
content with little.*

PLATO

CHAPTER THIRTEEN

$200,000? YOU'VE GOT TO BE KIDDING!

The average cost of attending public colleges now exceeds $10,000 per year. For private colleges and universities, it is a staggering $25,000 or more annually. Do you have enough money saved to send your child to college next year? What about five years from now or ten or twenty? If you have a one year old right now, your cash requirement for sending your child to college in seventeen years will be a whopping $285,000!

If you question whether or not you want to provide a college education for your children, you should know that according to census data, the average person with a bachelor's degree earns 73 percent more over a lifetime than a person with a high school diploma—and economists tell us the gap is growing.

If you have not planned for a "college investment account," it is time for you to close this educational gap.

One way to provide the best for your child is through a college education. Barry Habib, a financial advisor featured on CNBC offers this advice:

A family with a three-year-old child may have concerns about how it will meet future college expenses. A family that draws equity from its home today and invests those dollars with the help of a financial expert should solve the problem. Historically, money invested in mutual funds has yielded an average return of 15 percent per year over time frames of ten years or longer. This means that your investment should double every five years. . . .

Often, this type of cash out can be combined with a lower interest rate or debt consolidation plan that actually reduces the family's overall monthly payments while funding the college education plan. This type of scenario can also have favorable tax consequences since the interest paid on the mortgage is . . . tax deductible.

Talk to your trusted advisor about these two additional tips for funding a college education:

TIP 1: START EARLY. Start planning for your child's college education when you are pregnant.

TIP 2: TALK TO THE GRANDPARENTS. Most of the nation's wealth today is in this sector. Grandparents can receive financial benefits when they help with their grand-children's education.

CHAPTER FOURTEEN

MY MORTGAGE IS KILLING ME

Your home is your greatest financial asset, but your mortgage is also your largest debt. Most people who own homes are paying between 25 to 35 percent of their monthly paycheck toward their mortgage. Unfortunately, about 95 percent of Americans who own homes do not ask this important question: *Am I treating my mortgage as part of my financial plan?* In other words, are you working for your mortgage, or is your mortgage working for you?

Millions of people pay more interest than they should and endure higher rates than they should, all for longer periods than necessary. This can result in tens of thousands of dollars in unnecessary interest, which could go to better use in a financial plan. If you have never had a mortgage review, and if you are not sure if your loan meets with your overall financial objectives, here are three proven ways to help you close the gap.

Before you do anything, ask a professional mortgage consultant for a mortgage review. Though few lenders actually provide this no-cost service, the top professionals offer it annually.

When reviewing your mortgage, consider these three top strategies for mortgage management:

STRATEGY 1: REFINANCE FOR A LOWER PAYMENT OR AN OVERALL LOWER COST. Which is most important to you: the *rate* or the *overall lowest cost* for the loan? If it is rate, there is a good chance you can lower it by refinancing.

STRATEGY 2: ACCELERATE YOUR PAYMENTS. This strategy is one of the greatest financial management tools available to you, and you can do it in one of four ways: (1) Pay one extra payment a year—that is, pay twenty-six biweekly payments (equivalent to thirteen monthly payments) instead of twelve monthly payments, (2) Pay your thirty-year mortgage as if it were a fifteen-year loan, (3) Pay a fifteen-year mortgage as if it were a ten-year loan, or (4) Pay your adjustable-rate mortgage as if it were a fixed rate. Although your equity will earn only the percentage of appreciation within your real estate market, you will gain financial well-being.

You can also accelerate your payments by channeling "additional payments" into a "mortgage balance account." Each month, put money into in a mutual fund or some other account that will pay you a safe 10 to 15 percent. Let this build as your safeguard so that if an emergency occurs, you can reduce your mortgage dramatically with funds from this account. With this strategy in place, you earn an interest rate differential of 3 to 7 percent—that's the advantage. The disadvantage: Your principal does not go down as fast, thus your interest payments are higher for longer.

STRATEGY 3: PAY YOUR PROPERTY TAXES AND INSURANCE PAYMENTS YOURSELF. If your lender collects these yearly expenses each month from your mortgage payment, then you are not earning interest on that money. Tell your lender that you want your payments to be *principal and interest only*. Then open a "taxes and insurance account" with a money market or CD rate and make deposits into that account each month, just as you would to the lender. When you pay your real estate tax and homeowner's insurance bill, draw from that account and keep the interest, which, depending on your real estate taxes and insurance premiums, could be between $250 and $500 per year. With these overall savings, you and your family can experience more enjoyment in life and less overall financial stress.

> *We make a living*
> *by what we get,*
> *we make a life*
> *by what we give.*
>
> WINSTON CHURCHILL

CHAPTER FIFTEEN

TOO ENCUMBERED TO CARE

here is a piece of doggerel that says, *He who does only that which he is paid for will wonder someday what on earth he was made for.* Great walls of wealth can be effective when it comes to keeping out the sadness and pain that surround us. But those same walls can also filter out the satisfaction that comes from touching the lives of others. You will never be a complete success as a human if you keep your wealth to yourself. If you need a quick start in this area of philanthropy, here are a few ideas to help you close the gap.

When you die, how much of your money are you going to leave behind? The answer: *All of it.* Shrouds have no pockets.

Suze Orman, best-selling author of *The 9 Steps to Financial Freedom,* has an insightful outlook on money. She says, "I believe that each one of us is, in effect, a glass, in that we can hold only so much; after that, the water—or money—just goes down the drain."

The Bible teaches us about giving and is best represented by what is known as the *law of sowing and reaping.* Here are some verses that explain that law:

• "The generous soul will be made rich, and he who waters will also be watered himself" (Prov. 11:25).

• "It is more blessed to give than to receive" (Acts 20:35).

• "Do not be deceived . . . for whatever a mans sows, that he will also reap" (Gal. 6:7).

My friend and mentor Zig Ziglar says, "You can have everything you want in life if you just help enough other people get what they want." This is the principle of reciprocity, and it is as reliable as the law of gravity.

How much you earn is not important. How much you give is. Surprisingly, a recent government survey stated that those earning less than $10,000 a year give away 5.5 percent of their income to charitable causes; those earning over $500,000 a year give less than 3 percent.

Here are some questions that may prompt you to be more generous with what you have:

- How can I tithe more of the money God has blessed me with to my place of worship?
- On whom can I bestow my money so that it makes the biggest difference?
- What charitable organizations share my own goals and objectives?

If you want to feel good, then use your wealth to make others feel good.

Feel for others—

in your pocket.

CHARLES SPURGEON

SPIRITUAL ABUNDANCE

*To the heart
that is attuned to Him,
God comes in
surprising ways.*

HENRY GARIEPY

CHAPTER SIXTEEN

TOO BUSY TO PRAY

R ecent surveys indicate that more than 90 percent of Americans own at least one Bible. Eighty-six percent call themselves Christians. Of 1,012 adults surveyed in a July 1997 study by Barna Research, two out of three (67 percent) said they believe God is the all-knowing, all-powerful Creator of the universe who rules the world today. Is it possible that this same God has a plan for your life? Most people I know want to find direction through prayer, but they either do not have the time or don't know how to pray—or both. If you are not sure about when and how to pray, then it is time to close the gap in your communication with God.

"Nothing is more important. It's the source of life's greatest joy. There's no power or peace without it. With it, we receive supernatural insight and wisdom."

UNITED STATES SENATE CHAPLIN LLOYD JOHN OGILVIE

Try prayer. It changes things—and people.

A small boy once asked his parents, "I'm going to pray now—do you need anything?" With childlike faith, the boy believed that time spent in prayer would bring about the results he wanted. Somewhere along the road to becoming adults, however, many of us have lost our passion for time alone with God.

Here are three powerful ideas to help stimulate your prayer life:

1. BLOCK THE TIME. Have you noticed that we seem to stress about not having time for everything? However, the God of the universe tells us not to worry because He will care for us (Matt. 6:25–34).

Here are seven areas you may want to expore as you develop an effective prayer life:

- Union with God
- Focus on God
- God's plan for your life
- Daily provision
- Forgiveness for your wrong actions
- Protection from evil
- A celebration of your relationship with God

2. LISTEN TO HIS VOICE. When you pray, bring the issues of your life to God and say, "Father, speak to me. Tell me what you want for my life." Then listen—perhaps as long as fifteen minutes, even though it may seem like an eternity. Soon you will feel God nudging you, saying, *This is the way you should go.*

3. PRAY ABOUT EVERYTHING. The apostle Paul says that we are to "pray without ceasing" (1 Thess. 5:17). Why? Because you and I are not strong enough to carry out life's tough choices alone. Pray "situational prayers"—throughout the day, take any situation in which you need guidance to God in a short prayer.

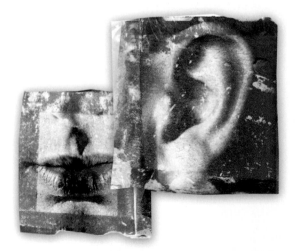

> *Prayer is a means*
> *God uses to give us*
> *what He wants.*
>
> W. BINGHAM HUNTER

CHAPTER SEVENTEEN

CAN'T SLOW DOWN— GOIN' TOO FAST

"*God made us plain and simple, but we have made ourselves very complicated.*" ECCLESIASTES 7:29, TEV

Ever feel like you are living your life on a treadmill . . . going fast, but nowhere in particular? You know you want to get off and take a breathier, but you can't? Have you traded peace of mind for a piece of the action? Are you so busy making a living that you are missing out on building a life? Do you know in your heart that there must be a better way? If you answered "yes" to any of these questions, then you are in the danger zone. It is time to close the gap before you do further damage to your body and your brain.

Pastor and author Chuck Swindoll says it like this: ". . . the need to simplify is imperative. Otherwise, we will find ourselves unable to be at rest within, unable to enter the deep, silent resources of our hearts, where God's best messages are communicated."

Most people I know don't know how to simplify. Somehow we have equated *busy* with *success* and *accumulation* with *contentment.* Here are two practical steps to help you reorder your life:

STEP 1: MAKE NEW CHOICES. To simplify, we must make new choices by reconnecting with what is important to us. Begin by asking yourself these questions:

• What activities or relationships do I need to eliminate to be able to slow down? How and when can I make these changes?

• What areas of my life do I really value? What would my life look like if these areas received serious attention?

STEP 2: ENGAGE IN SOLITUDE WITH GOD. Spiritual abundance comes from knowing that you are experiencing God in a meaningful way, and that your actions are a reflection of those moments of solitude with Him.

Thomas Merton says, "Solitude is not something you must hope for in the future. Rather, it is a deepening of the present." Are you living life to its fullest? If not, spend some time alone with God.

CHAPTER EIGHTEEN

WHERE IS GOD WHEN I NEED HIM?

 here was God when my child died?

Where was God when my spouse left me?

Where was God when I received the news that I was terminally ill?

Where was God when the business deal went south?

Many people ask, "Where was God when I needed him?" Or "If God were here, this never would have happened." But if we were honest, we would look for God's presence all around us, and we would listen for what God is teaching us in our present situation. Let's work at closing the gap of blaming God.

In July 1989, I heard Zig Ziglar speak at a church service; his words had a "laser impact" on my life. He said that the God of the universe—the Creator—looks out for us on a full-time basis, but we often lack the same commitment in return.

Think about it. He is infinitely more interested in your life than you are. Everything and anything that happens in your life is part of His plan for you. So, when bad things happen, remember these points.

• God loves us, and His plan is best. The Scriptures say that "God is love" and ". . . perfect love casts out fear" (1 John 4:8, 18). He loves us so much that He gave us the ultimate gift, His Son.

• God is smarter than we are, and His direction is accurate. The Scriptures say that God will continue to perfect us to the end (Phil. 1:6).

• God is more powerful than we are, and He will help us through the tough times. He does not remove the hurt, but He *does* provide us with strength for our trials—He sent us a helper, the Holy Spirit.

When you suffer pain or loss, don't say that God is *no where*. Instead, change the position of just one letter, and believe that your heavenly Father is *now here*.

CHAPTER NINETEEN

I FEEL SO ALONE!

Max Lucado has written these comforting words: "God is for you. Not 'may be,' not 'has been,' not 'was,' not 'would be,' but 'God is!' He is for you today. At this hour. At this minute."

And, I would add, He is here to help you close the spiritual gaps in your life, especially during those times when you feel so desperately alone. God says, "For where two or three are gathered together in My name, I am there in the midst of them" (Matt. 18:20) and "a threefold cord is not quickly broken" (Eccles. 4:12). With these words of encouragement, you can know that there is a power to help you survive and thrive—it comes from other people. God has designed some proven master principles that will lead you through lonely moments; He will help you close the gap.

"As iron sharpens iron, so a man sharpens the countenance of his friend." PROVERBS 27:17

Your friends can help you find peace when you feel alone, abandoned, uncertain, or afraid. Friends with spiritual discernment can provide you with wisdom and clarity, helping you to see things about God's ministry that you are unable to see. They can give you hope during life's most difficult moments.

The psalmist David said, "Yea, though I walk through the valley of the shadow of death, I will fear no evil; for you are with me; your rod and your staff, they comfort me" (Ps. 23:4). All of life's challenges are transitional, not permanent—you are going *through* them. The essential question is, Are you also *growing* through your struggles?

Here are several steps that will help you deal effectively with difficult transitions and decisions.

• **Don't go it alone.** Everyone needs a friend during tough times. There is as much benefit in being a friend as in having a friend. Who are the top two or three friends you can count on to help you through difficult times? Do they know you have selected them for such an important role in your life? If not, call them today, and let them know how special they are to you.

• **Find an accountability partner.** Each Friday, I speak with my accountability partner. He asks me questions about how I am handling issues in my life. As humans, we often create our own "valleys," but we can learn to have fewer of them when we perform well in areas of faith. When I fail, my friend has compassion on me and helps me to get back on track. He has no pretense, no ulterior motive. He simply cares for me and wants me to succeed.

- **Get involved in a covenant or small group.** Covenant groups were founded in the early 1600s when Presbyterians sought to create a vehicle that would extend and preserve their faith. In modern times, they fulfill much the same role; these groups are made up of people who meet regularly to discuss issues that are important to the entire group.

Small groups provide a forum for releasing pent-up emotions, encouraging right behavior, and promoting a love that transcends boundaries of performance.

There is divine purpose

in bringing out the

best in one another.

DENIS WAITLEY

CHAPTER TWENTY

NOTHING HAPPENED TODAY

T hroughout Scripture, God warns His people to remember Him. Still, it did not take long for the Israelites to forget that He gave them safe passage across the Red Sea, furnished their daily bread, and provided reliable daily and nightly guides on their journey in pillars of cloud and fire.

God was serious when He asked the Israelites to construct monuments and memorials to Him. He not only wanted them to remember His mighty deeds in the past, but He also sought to inspire them to trust Him in the future. What parts of your spiritual life demand "stones of remembrance"? Are you making notes of your joys and struggles? Are you jotting down the details of how God is working in your life? If not, here is a proven way to help you create lasting memories that will close the gap of selective forgetfulness.

Journaling is powerful. Your journal can be a personal history book of how God has worked and is working in your life. When you write in your journal, you create a vital intimacy with God that augments your capacity to trust Him.

My friend Daniel Harkavy, president of Building Champions, a personal coaching company, says that journaling offers these benefits:

• **It increases thanksgiving.** By recording the lessons that God has taught you today, you gain a heart of thankfulness for the distance He has brought you.

• **It ingrains the lesson.** Journaling imprints lessons into our minds and increases the impact of those lessons, especially if we constantly review them.

• **It enhances our lives.** Through journaling, we can better assess how our life is progressing. It can bring clarity that enables us to make better decisions.

• **It quiets our hearts.** Serenity is a by-product of journaling. Life is too short *not* to hear the quiet whisper of God. Feeling His presence while journaling is one of the most powerful forms of abundance.

• **It leaves a road map.** When we record what we have received and learned from God, we are creating a road map for our children and friends to follow.

CHAPTER TWENTY-ONE

HUMBLE . . .
AND PROUD OF IT

Humility is a strange animal. The moment we think we have it, we have lost it. Martin Luther once wrote, "God creates out of nothing. Therefore until a man is nothing, God can make nothing out of him." His point is well-taken. However, who among us chooses to surrender willingly our strengths, abilities, and our power—especially our *will*power? It's not easy. Here's the rub: the moment we *think* we know a lot about something, peace departs and leaves us orphaned in spirit. Let's close the gap of humility.

I recently finished a seminar in Hawaii. As I watched the peaceful waters of the blue Pacific from my hotel window, I thought of a seminar I gave years earlier. My business was dangling over the edge of financial collapse, and I learned a lesson of humility in a big way. At the end of the event, I read an evaluation that said, "Todd is full of himself." Ouch!

I must tell you: while I did not intentionally exalt myself, apparently one of my clients thought I had. I try to own a spirit of humility, but I find myself always having to keep it in check. The root of this problem for me is pride—a sense of superiority. And I know I'm not alone.

IS HUMILITY WORTH PURSUING?

- It is the road to honor.   1 KINGS 3:11–14
- It leads to riches.   PROVERBS 22:4
- It unlocks God's grace.   PROVERBS 3:34 and JAMES 4:6
- It insures God's presence.   ISAIAH 57:15

HOW DO YOU ACHIEVE THIS HUMBLE SPIRIT?

- Put on a "new self."   COLOSSIANS 3:1–13
- Clothe yourself with humility.   1 PETER 5:5
- Walk rightly.   1 JOHN 2:6

Humility is a function of God's presence in our lives. Jesus' words will ultimately close the gap: "So the last will be first, and the first last" (Matt. 20:16).

*Mountains cannot
be surmounted except
by winding paths.*
JOHANN W. VON GOETHE

CHAPTER TWENTY-TWO

WHAT LEGACY?

My friend Denis Waitley, author and speaker on achievement, says, "People often spend more time planning their vacations and holidays than they spend planning their life." Denis is right. Most people do not think much about centering their lives around a purposeful plan that insures their legacy—they do not reflect on that lasting, final impression they will make on their family, community, business associates, and church. Why? Perhaps because they feel they have too little to offer. They are not famous or wealthy, and they do not possess so-called "star" qualities. Well, let's forget about making *Who's Who,* or the cover of *People Magazine,* and begin thinking about your family and friends—those nearest and dearest to you. What lasting impression do you hope to leave on their lives? If you would like some practical assistance in the legacy-leaving department, here are some ways to close the gap.

I have a drawer in my office reserved for my kids. It is a "treasure chest" I am leaving for them. For the rest of my life, I will pass out trinkets from this drawer—visual and emotional reminders of what I believe in and what I want them to remember from me. Building a legacy for my family is part of my life plan. I am doing it on purpose and *with a purpose.*

In my book, *The Power to Be Your Best!,* I include a story about Robert E. Lee. On a snowy day, long before the Civil War, Lee took his eight-year-old son, Custis, out for a walk. The boy, wearied by the high drifts, began to fall behind his father. After a few minutes, Lee looked back and saw that Custis was behind him, imitating his every move and walking in his tracks. "When I saw this," Lee told one of his friends long afterward, "I said to myself, 'It behooves me to walk very straight when this fellow is already following in my footsteps.'"

What is in your "treasure chest?" How are you creating a legacy? Here are some practical ideas for legacy building:

IDEA 1: THE FINAL FRAME. How do you want to be remembered by those you love most? I am referring to the heart and soul of what you stand for, the lessons you have taught, and how you have demonstrated your convictions. What does your "final frame" look like? The good news is that you still have time to begin living a life consistent with that final picture.

IDEA 2: THE DAILY DISCIPLINE. Make a list of your convictions. Include the attitudes you want to display and the things you want to communicate so that you can discipline yourself to do these things more consistently.

IDEA 3: ETERNAL IMPACT. Make a difference— forever. Your spiritual decisions impact both your life and the lives of those you love. Even though life has a 100 percent mortality rate, the good news is that you *can* be certain of your next stop. Ask yourself, "When I finally depart this earthly scene, where will I go?" What about those you love . . . will they join you?

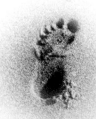

Open your spiritual

treasure chest today,

and dig deep.

PETER WALLACE

VOCATIONAL
EXELLENCE

Whatever you are,

be a good one.

ABRAHAM LINCOLN

CHAPTER TWENTY-THREE

HELP!
I HATE MY JOB!

Monotony can be the breeding ground for envy and discontent, or it can be the training ground for the development of character and a life of service. It all depends on whether we can see God in the ordinary duties of life. I once heard about a cleaning lady who worked in the same office building for forty years. One day, she was interviewed by a reporter who asked her how she could stand doing the same humdrum tasks, day in and day out. The women gave this reply: "Oh, I don't get bored. I use cleaning material that God made. I clean objects that belong to people God made, and I make life more comfortable for them. My mop is in the hand of God!"

How about you? Do you dislike your job, can't get along with your boss? Do you have a sinking feeling that you have missed the vocational boat? Are you struggling to find a way out of your boredom? If so, then let's close the gap.

Do what you love, love what you do, and do it
well. The best way not to be bored on your job is to choose a
job that isn't boring.

The Scriptures tell us that our mind plans the way but
that *God directs our steps* (Prov. 16:9). Is your vocation in alignment with what God wants for you? Here is a formula that
may help you find the right path:

Follow the "Triple AAA bc" formula. My friend Glenna
Salsbury, author of *The Art of the Fresh Start*, says if you are
bored and do not like your job, you can . . .

• Alter your current work experience by changing
departments, or if you are unemployed, consider a completely
different field.

• Avoid your current employment, perhaps by resigning.

• Accept your current situation if the financial risk is too
great to warrant quitting at this time. In the meantime,

    * build your strengths by developing other passions, and

    * change your perspective by planning your next
career, complete with timelines.

God placed on my heart that one day I would be a speaker,
but I could not afford to leave my job to become one. I used
Glenna's formula: I accepted my current situation while
planning my speaking career. Five years later, I was ready,
and I never experienced boredom again.

CHAPTER TWENTY-FOUR

SO MUCH TO DO, SO LITTLE TIME

"*To everything there is a season, a time for every purpose under heaven.*" ECCLESIASTES 3:1

How well do you manage your time? Are you so organized that you can deliver what you promise to others, as well as what you promise to yourself? Can you look in the mirror at night and say, "I used my time to the fullest today"? When you make commitments to your family, friends, and associates, do you deliver? If your time-management solutions are not working for you, the good news is that help is only a few words away. Here are three tested ways to help you close the gap.

Time management is a waste of time! Now do I have your attention? For most people, time management is much like raking water: lots of movement, with little, if any, results.

The only way to live your life to the fullest is through *life-productive behavior*—something best served by engaging in the following action thoughts.

- **Values clarity.** Name five things that are important to you. To commit to those areas, you'll need to create an environment that effectively uses your time. When your activities are aligned with what is significant to you, you can have inner peace. And high levels of inner peace reduce stress.

We should spend at least fifteen minutes a day—in one sitting—discovering how we can find fulfillment in one or more of these areas. Roy Disney said, "When values are clear, decisions are easy."

- **The art of time blocking.** Your values depend upon time blocking. You cannot manage your time with Post-it notes, scribbled "to-do" checklists, or electronic gadgetry. Instead, you must decide in advance what your day will look like. Then you must discipline yourself to focus on the particular activities you set in your "time blocks," or segments of time. These activities, or "events," are linked to what you value, which results in a clearer, less-cluttered schedule and increased levels of motivation to do the event.

CHAPTER TWENTY-FIVE

WHY DOES EVERYBODY SAY "NO"?

O ver a half million salespeople say they have experienced "call reluctance." For as long as they have been selling, they have heard the word *no* more than the word *yes* when trying to move a buyer to action. Still, they have been told at one or more ineffective sales sessions, "Don't worry. Just remember that rejection is part of the game." This is often followed by the counsel, "Every 'no' moves you one step closer to a 'yes' . . . just keep trying. It's only a matter of time." Armed with this inept philosophy, the salespeople discover their customers and business associates move even *further* away from "yes."

Do you want your prospects to meet with you more readily? Do you want your boss to say "yes" to your proposals more frequently? Read on, for you are about to receive the "stealth weapon" of influence.

"The generous soul will be made rich. He who waters others will himself be watered." PROVERBS 11:25

There are two essential ideas to the art of influence: adding value and understanding the motivation to buy. Ignoring either of these can create resistance, which typically results in a longer sales cycle or no sale at all. Ask yourself, "Am I a salesperson, or am I a trusted advisor?"

Whenever the product gets into the hundreds-of-dollars range, you must become a trusted advisor. Remember that resistance *decreases* when trust *increases*. To make this happen, follow these steps:

• **Add value.** Whenever you ask prospects to meet with you, buy from you, or refer you to someone else, *give them something of value.* When I learned this at the age of twenty-three, my sales nearly tripled.

• **Master the values conversation.** My friend Bill Bachrach, author of *Values-Based Selling: The Art of Building High-Trust Client Relationships*, has built his professional career around one central question, "What's important about ———— to you?" First, put your product in the blank. Then, repeat this question one or more times using your client's answer(s) in the blank. This will help you discover their real motivation for obtaining your product or service—this is the motivation to buy. If you link your product or service to this motivation, you will create acceptance and trust.

People buy feelings, not features and benefits. Remember that a camera leads to memories, a house leads to security, an insurance policy leads to protection, and on and on. Master this, and you will enjoy security forever.

Failure is the greatest

opportunity to know

who I really am.

JOHN KILLINGER

CHAPTER TWENTY-SIX

THE CUSTOMER IS ALWAYS . . . *WHAT?*

The truism goes, "The customer is always right!" But I marvel at the paradox of much of today's customer service. Every business needs customers to survive, yet most employees fail to understand that their paycheck and long-term job security are related to customer relationships—how customers feel about the employees' interaction with them.

Have you ever erupted into a storm of defensiveness when a customer did not give you the feedback you desired? Do you completely reject any "negative" view of your performance? If you answered "yes" to either question, then perhaps I can provide some insight that may help you close this gap.

"You can shear a sheep for many years, but you may skin it only once." JOHN SEWELL

You cannot afford to lose customers. Here are the top four strategies for building customer loyalty:

STRATEGY 1: "LIFETIME" THEM. A car buyer can have a lifetime worth of $300,000 to a car dealership. Someone who buys food from a grocery store can have a lifetime value of over $350,000 to the grocer. How much are your customers worth to you?

STRATEGY 2: UNDERPROMISE; OVERDELIVER. Customers keep coming back when they know you will exceed their expectations. Here's the rule: give it to them faster and for less money than they expected. Add true value. Most businesses do it backwards: they promise fast service but deliver slow and quote less but charge more.

STRATEGY 3: BEFORE THEY PAY, SURVEY. Do not wait until your buyers have made their purchases to ask how you did. That's too late. Ask them *before they buy*. If there are any issues you have overlooked, you can fix them before finalizing the bill.

STRATEGY 4: WHEN THEY'RE MAD, MAKE 'EM HAPPY. When your performance delivers less than a customer expects, do something about it—*recover*. Companies must train and empower their employees to recover customers, and when they do, the customer will return . . . again and again.

CHAPTER TWENTY-SEVEN

GROUNDED BY THE FOG

If you've ever spent time in London, enjoyed a weekend in San Francisco, or driven down Highway 99 on the way to Fresno, California, then you know what it is like to inch your way through a blanket of fog. Fog debilitates. It slows you down. You think you know what lies ahead, but when the fog clears, you are surprised by the reality of your surroundings. If you pretend the fog is not a problem—and you maintain your speed—you will meet disaster head-on. It is the same with leadership. If your vision is "foggy" and you refuse to acknowledge your challenges, then you're putting you and your team in jeopardy—and your future is most certainly on the brink of disaster. If you are working in such a fog-bound environment, let's clear the air and close the gap.

Listen to these words from my friend John Maxwell, author and motivational speaker:

"My observation over the last twenty years has been that all effective leaders have a vision of what they must accomplish. That vision becomes the energy behind every effort and the force that pushes through all the problems."

Here are four practical strategies for integrating vision into your team or company:

STRATEGY 1: THE VISION MUST BE BACKED BY THE INTEGRITY OF THE LEADER. People must buy into the leader before they will ever buy into the vision.

STRATEGY 2: VISIONS MUST HAVE PURPOSE. This is the "why" in the organization. Starting today, get clear on why you are in business. Then tie your vision to your purpose, and make it happen. Vision and purpose must be compatible.

STRATEGY 3: VISIONS MUST BE FAR-REACHING BUT ATTAINABLE. My friend Mike Vance worked alongside Walt Disney until Walt's death. Mike told me that Disney never came up with a vision that was too far away from reality. In fact, the Disney Company is still working on some of Walt's visions forty years after his death.

STRATEGY 4: VISIONS MUST BE PUBLIC. Before a team can accomplish a vision, they must know where their leader is going. In return, with team feedback, most leaders can count on faster, more efficient progress.

CHAPTER TWENTY-EIGHT

I DID IT;
WHY CAN'T THEY?

The following statement is one of the greatest secrets of effective leadership: *We shall no longer strive for our own way but commit ourselves, honestly and simply, to inspiring others to develop the power to be their best.* Hardly the stereotypical spirit of the legendary, tough-minded CEO! But if leadership is a challenge for you, then you must begin to lead by that statement. If you are constantly dealing with others not measuring up to your self-compared expectations, if you are pushing your team members down rather than pulling them up, and if you want overall better performance from your team, now is the time to close the gap.

Are you holding others back, or are you inspiring them to win?

Leadership is all about influence and motivation. Neither happens naturally, but they are both the results of intentional leadership decisions. As a leader, you must recognize that your role is not a title. *Leadership is a position.* You must realize that people came to work for you *not to make you successful,* but *to become more successful themselves.* You must understand that the team is more important than you are and that the team needs to receive the credit for your success. How does a leader deploy these truths? Follow these ideas:

IDEA 1: LEADERSHIP IS INFLUENCE. People always do things for *their* reasons, not yours. Leaders must develop an environment that helps team members thrive, while still moving them to higher levels of "followership."

IDEA 2: MASTER MOTIVATION. Recent studies provide several big motivators for higher levels of performance: significant contributions, goal and quota participation, positive dissatisfaction (knowing you can do better), recognition, and clear expectations. The same studies tell us that the big de-motivators include belittling, manipulation, discouragement, lack of personal growth, and a condescending leader.

About 50 percent of your leadership challenges will dissipate when you raise the bar—and close the gap—in the areas of influence and motivation.

RIGHT JOB, WRONG PERSON

Most of the time, when you hire someone, you've done your homework. You checked references, and you possibly even reviewed the results of psychological testing. You also relied on the most direct evidence of all: You could look the new employee in the eye and say, *Yes! This is the one.*

But then . . . disaster struck. Round peg in a square hole. Suddenly, you were in trouble, and you asked yourself, *How could this happen?* You probably weren't ready to shoulder the responsibility for the result, but you forced yourself to accept your poor decision. Did you know that two out of the three reasons employers hire the wrong person are the fault of the employer? If this has ever happened to you, and you do not want it to happen again, then it is time to close this employee gap.

If you want your organization to thrive,

then you must master the process of selecting and hiring of the right people.

TIP 1: KNOW PRECISELY WHO YOU ARE LOOKING FOR. Don't just describe the scope of the position—identify the characteristics of the candidate.

TIP 2: RECRUIT PEOPLE WHO ARE ALREADY SUCCESSFULLY EMPLOYED. The people you really want—the best people—already have jobs. They are not perusing the Help-Wanted ads.

TIP 3: USE TRIPLE INTERVIEWS TO GET THE REAL INNER-VIEW. Deploy the *three meeting approach* to hiring. Meeting #1—Ask questions that test for the five characteristics you are looking for. (Top organizations look for these characteristics: integrity and character, the right fit, energy, intelligence, and a proven and successful track record.) Spend ninety percent of your time listening. Meeting #2—Spend equal time asking and listening. Meeting #3—Spend ninety percent of your time presenting the contract, salary, benefits, and training package. Then get them to buy-in.

TIP 4: GET THEM OFF TO THE RIGHT START. The first days and weeks on the job set the stage for your new hire's entire career with you. Take the time to introduce them to their teammates. Allocate time to train them in your company's culture and procedures and their job tasks—never assume they can "hit the street running."

CHAPTER THIRTY

WEED EATER WANTED

I f you have a flower garden, then you know that weeds are not respecters of the seasons. They thrive year-round, raising their unwanted heads between rocks, masquerading as the tender plants that you carefully nurture. However, they are still weeds, and they must be dealt with before they take over your garden. It is the same with leadership. If you discover you have *weeds* in your place of employment—people who pretend to be effective but are not—then you have two choices. You can either ignore the problem and hope it goes away (it won't), or you can become a *weed eater* and take control. If you feel you could use some insight in this area, here are some tools to help you close the gap.

I have worked closely with hundreds of leaders who laugh when confronted with this business truth: *don't water the weeds!* Here are some ideas for *pulling those weeds*:

IDEA 1: BACK TO THE BASICS. Long ago, Vilfredo Pareto, an Italian statistician, said that 20 percent of the people in an organization are responsible for 80 percent of a company's success. Under this principle then, you should:

• Spend 80 percent of your time with the top 20 percent of your people.

• Spend 80 percent of your training dollars on this top 20 percent.

• Ask the top 20 percent to mentor the next 20 percent, then watch this 40 percent outperform the previous 100 percent.

IDEA 2: PARTNERSHIP PLANNING. There are four types of employees: (1) High profit, high maintenance; (2) low profit, high maintenance; (3) high profit, low maintenance; and (4) low profit, low maintenance. Your goal as a leader is to terminate the top two, retain the third, and develop the fourth. You can accomplish this with vision and coaching: let your team know where you are going and help them get there by developing their skills.

IDEA 3: HELP THEM QUIT. Set a deadline for how long you will coach high-maintenance employees, letting them know that if they do not improve within that period, they will be terminated.

CHAPTER THIRTY-ONE

CAN'T I JUST FAKE IT?

George Burns, the cigar-champing comic who outlived almost everyone in his generation—including his doctors—was once asked the secret of his enduring success. After taking a couple of long drags on his stogy, Burns thought a bit and answered, "That's easy. The secret of my success is integrity."

"Integrity, so that's it," the reporter responded.

"Yeah, integrity," said Burns, flashing his wry smile. "And if you can fake that, you've got it made!"

That's a clever one-liner, but you and I both know it won't fly in the real world of business and relationships. Okay, reality check: Are you playing a game of pretend when it comes to living a life of integrity . . . hoping that no one will discover your real agenda? If so, you may be able to fake it for awhile, but rather than risk ultimate disaster, wouldn't it be better to use the present window of opportunity to close the gap?

"He who walks with integrity walks securely, but he who perverts his ways will become known." PROVERBS 10:9

The Scriptures speak in detail about integrity. Integrity guides us, restores us, builds our reputation, and secures our legacy. Integrity makes good business sense. Companies that achieve long-term success display the kind of integrity that customers and employees can count on.

Are you a person of integrity? Are you a person who keeps your word to yourself and others? Here is why integrity is so important:

BENEFIT 1: INCREASED SELF-ESTEEM. When you are a person of integrity, you feel better about yourself as a person. When you feel good about you, you will be more effective with those you lead.

BENEFIT 2: EMPLOYEE PRODUCTIVITY AND LOYALTY. With employees, your integrity translates into trust. When employees have confidence in you, their commitment will be without limits.

BENEFIT 3: MAINTAINING A CLEAR CONSCIENCE. One of the great benefits to leading with integrity is a clear conscience. A clear, honest mind gives you the power to lead with conviction.

BENEFIT 4: PROFESSIONAL MOMENTUM AND ADVANCEMENT. You want to continue to advance to higher levels of excellence. The highest level of leadership is when people follow you because they respect you and what you represent.

CHAPTER THIRTY-TWO

TOO BUSY WORKING TO DO WHAT I LOVE

ature requires balance. The most high-tech aircraft or space vehicle demands balance. A performer on a high-wire lives or dies by balance. Our physical bodies beg for balance.

Being overly absorbed with work makes us lopsided and weakens our spirit. The average person, on his or her deathbed, will not say, *"I wish I had spent more time at the computer—or shuffling paper."* So the question is: Where are you in the balance department? Are you too busy at the office to spend time with your spouse, your children, your neighbors, your friends— or with God? If you are a workaholic, or pushing hard for this certificate of demerit, here are some innovative ways to help you to begin closing the gap.

Here are ten ways to help you enjoy more balance in your life—starting today:

1. SCHEDULE IT. Balance is not something that happens after work and on weekends. It must become routine.

2. DELEGATE. You lose many hours because you do not delegate effectively on the job. What are you doing that an assistant could do?

3. PRAY AND MEDITATE. Don't look down; look up. Pursue spiritual harmony and peace. For me, this is private time with my Creator.

4. DATE YOUR SPOUSE. A leader I coached told me that he recently dated his wife for the first time in twenty-one years, and it rejuvenated their relationship.

5. HANG OUT WITH YOUR KIDS. Don't just "be there"; spend quality time with them.

6. WALK ON THE BEACH. Or any other beautiful place. Take time to be tranquil.

7. WORK OUT. Exercise enhances your physical and emotional health. Do it least three days a week.

8. TAKE A VACATION OR A DAY OFF. Sharpen the saw. You must be sharp to lead.

9. GET A MASSAGE. RELAX TO RECHARGE. Every month, get a good massage to release the stress and toxins that have built up in your body.

10. READ A GOOD BOOK. Put your brain in neutral on occasion.

FAMILY
MATTERS

*A happy
family is but an
earlier heaven.*

SIR JOHN BOWRING

CHAPTER THIRTY-THREE

BEEN THERE; DONE THAT

E ven those who *stand in love* (the mature afterglow of *falling in love*) can take their spouses for granted because familiarity can breed distance—and boredom. If a "spirit of ho-hum" has settled into your relationship, then you may already be in trouble. This is the time when we become possessive, rude, and insensitive to our mate. Dating our beloved becomes the farthest thing from our minds. Big mistake! Let's take inventory. How alive is your relationship with the one you love? Do you block out time on your calendar to be with your spouse? Is he or she the most important person in your life? If so, do your actions show it? Or are your words hollow? If you need a nudge to help you close what may be a widening gap, then read on.

Think back to when it all started. Do you remember the first time you saw each other? How your heart raced at the thought of seeing each other again?

Making a strong marriage is hard work. Making it *exciting* doesn't happen accidentally. Marriage is not an act of convenience. It is a matter of commitment. What standards have we set for keeping our marriages strong? The answer comes in *demonstrated love*. There are ways we can make sure our spouse knows and fully experiences our love.

Dating says "I love you." Think for a moment of what you did, while you were dating, to fan the early flames of your relationship. Imagine what your relationship would look like if you did those same things today. Here's your checklist:

My spouse will know my love for him/her today because:

We spent some meaningful time together.	❏ Done
I asked questions that demonstrated my interest in him/her.	❏ Done
I really listened when my spouse talked.	❏ Done
I was courteous when we were together.	❏ Done
I was patient.	❏ Done
I was kind in both deed and word.	❏ Done
I was unselfish, putting his/her needs first.	❏ Done
I held to my commitments of time.	❏ Done
I forgave and asked for forgiveness.	❏ Done
I spoke and demonstrated my love in real ways.	❏ Done

CHAPTER THIRTY-FOUR

SINGLE AND FEELING UNLOVED

Eleanor Roosevelt wrote, "One must never, for whatever reason, turn one's back on life." What good counsel for us, especially for those who do not have a mate. A God who loves you more than you can possibly know has created you for a divine purpose. Yet, if you are without a partner, you may feel some of that God-inspired purpose has lost its edge. This is when you simply must believe that you are not here by accident. If, however, you still find it a challenge to go it alone in a "couples world," here are some ways to help you close the gap.

"But I say to the unmarried and to the widows: It is good for them if they remain even as I am." 1 CORINTHIANS 7:8

Do you think it's possible that being without a mate right now is God's plan for your life? Let me tell you a story. My dad's mom, Ellyene Enault, passed away at the age of ninety-six. She had a rich life, and for the last twenty years of it, she was without a mate. My mom's mom, Kathryn Burgess, is ninety-three and has been without a mate for more than fifty years. Both of these women have led rich and rewarding lives. Both made an impact on mine.

When I was younger, I was engaged to be married twice, but neither relationship worked out. Throughout this painful dating process, my nana Ellyene kept saying, "Todd, when it's right, you will know it. When the right woman appears, you won't have to force anything." She was right. I had to wait on God's timing, but in doing so, I found a wonderful wife, Sheryl, and we now have two beautiful boys, Jonathan and Matthew. I can't imagine my life without them.

If you are single today, there is hope. And that hope is in trusting God for His plan. The key is this: Don't put your life on hold while you wait.

- Become whole, take care of you, and pursue your purpose and excellence. The question, "Why am I here?" is tough to answer. It requires considerable introspection. When you come up with your answer, having a mate becomes secondary. Finding your purpose leads to actions that make you whole.

Your purpose can give you feelings of completeness and fulfillment. Find out everything you can about that special ingredient *in you* that enhances your self-worth.

• Relax. I have found that when people make relationship decisions from a position of stress, that relationship is less likely to survive. Relax. There are six billion people on this planet, and the chances are good that one of those people will be your mate. The comforting thought is that God already knows the outcome. Trust Him, go to His Word, and pray for His divine guidance in your life for this area.

• Reach out to others and add value. As a single person, be sure that your emotional and spiritual needs are met. One way to do this is to reach out to others. Whether one-on-one or in a group, focus on giving your time and energy to those who are in your circle—that is, add value to their lives. Your rewards will be more than you ever dreamed of, both personally and professionally.

God has given us
two hands—one for
receiving and the other
for giving.

BILLY GRAHAM

CHAPTER THIRTY-FIVE

INCHES OF DIFFERENCE

The idea of spending quality time with your children is something that has been blown out of proportion in our society. For one thing, it is a difficult concept to define. What may be quality time to one person may not be quality time for another. Most family experts now believe it is *what we do* in the time we spend with our children that counts. Period! The five-second hug . . . the ten minutes of play on the rug before you run off to an evening meeting . . . reading a two-minute story before leaving for work in the morning—these are just as important as the amount of time you spend with them. However, if you still feel pangs of guilt for not spending quality time with your children, according to your definition, here are few great ways to close the gap.

"Behold, children are a heritage from the Lord, the fruit of the womb is a reward." PSALM 127:3

No other parents spend less time with their children than Americans. According to *The Wall Street Journal*, American parents spend, on average, "less than fifteen minutes a week in serious discussions with their children." Recent reports from the National Center for Fathering indicate that fathers spend as little as thirty-seven seconds a day interacting with their children.

Effective parents spend time with their children, not only when they're young, but also when they're teens. A recent report from the Carnegie Council on Adolescent Development states, "Without the sustained involvement of parents and other adults . . . young adolescents are at risk of harming themselves and others . . . Many reach adulthood ill-equipped to participate responsibly in our society."

There is a difference between merely being a part of our children's lives and actively being *in* their lives. The difference is only "inches." The distance between passing in the hallway and hugging in the hallway is only inches, but what an impact that hug can make. The distance between telling your children to pray and getting on your knees and doing it with them is only inches, but how important those inches are.

CHAPTER THIRTY-SIX

EQUIPPING YOUR CHILDREN FOR EXCELLENCE

Y ou see them everywhere, in every possible way—children growing up. At every age, from birth to adulthood, their brains are bombarded with messages of how to act and react, how to love, how to hate, how to learn, what to say and how to say it, and how to live. These messages come flying at them relentlessly. Everyday, the forces of manipulation are in full swing to modify the way our children think, for both good and bad. However, too much of the "bad" is getting through.

Children everywhere are smoking, drinking, stealing, lying, killing, and falling into an almost never-ending tailspin of relativism. They have not internalized absolutes or the rules for *life-productive behavior.* If any of this sounds true about your children, then let's quickly close this gap.

"Train up a child in the way he should go, and when he is old he will not depart from it." PROVERBS 22:6

What hand have you dealt your kids? Have you given them a road map to life? Dr. Haim Ginot, a renowned child psychologist, says, "A parent's responsibility is not to his child's happiness; it's to character—it's equipping them for excellence." We need to get involved with our children's lives; we need to instruct them in the very fabric of spiritual, moral, ethical, and relational truth.

Here are four ideas to help you equip your kids:

1. MAKE A COMMITMENT. This is the first order of business. Our readiness and willingness to carry out our parenting responsibilities demonstrates our commitment to our children. Are you eager to be with them? Does spending time with them excite you? This commitment must to be honored daily. Give them your time, energy, and resources. Without hesitation, let them know you love them through deeds and words.

2. SET EXPECTATIONS AND BOUNDARIES. Parents without boundaries raise children without boundaries. What boundaries have you set for your children? Do they know your expectations? It may be as simple as teaching them to say "please" and "thank you" or as complex as setting the age for when they can begin to date or talking about the temptation of sexual involvement before marriage. Behind these seemingly difficult—even unfair—boundaries lie benefits that will last a lifetime for your kids.

3. BE A MODEL. "I don't hear you as loud as I see you," said a young boy to his father. What a wake-up call! If you do not model good boundary behavior, neither will your child.

4. BE ACCESSIBLE. Equipping your children for excellence means making sure they have the right answers to the tough questions. Let your children know you are there to listen to them—on their level. Show them you are approachable by "dating" them. As a young boy, I looked forward to one-on-one times with my dad. Whether it was hiking, fishing, or going the park, he always kept those dates; they were a priority. Your children can't share their deepest concerns with you if you aren't available to hear them. Open the door, and make a difference in their lives.

There are only two

lasting bequests we can

hope to give our children.

One of these is roots,

the other wings.

HOLDING CARTER

CHAPTER THIRTY-SEVEN

MY HOUSE . . . A CLASSROOM?

f your house were a classroom, what would you teach your children? Would your classes be interesting? What kind of teacher would you be? Would you take a personal interest in each child? Would you encourage them to realize their full potential . . . to develop the power to be their best? If this concept of making your house a classroom seems awkward, even strange, then there may be serious gaps in your relationships with your children. Let's close some of them with some proven-effective "out of the box" principles.

116

If you are like many parents, you do not have a classroom in your home. But consider this: A central place for learning not only accelerates the development of your children but also adds to the formal bonding necessary to family success.

My mentor, Mike Vance, has taught me things that will benefit me for the rest of my life, especially his Kitchen of the Mind™ concept. Mike decided to devote his living room solely to learning—a "kitchen for the mind"—and filled it with learning tools, such as a microscope, telescope, terrarium, talking globe, paints, encyclopedias, and electronic games.

From Mike, I have learned these three principles for developing a child's mind:

PRINCIPLE 1: HAVE FUN. Children love to learn. Become a child with your children. Make learning enjoyable.

PRINCIPLE 2: INTRODUCE NEW THINGS OFTEN. Start out small, but introduce new learning tools on a regular basis. If your child has a bent toward something, add it to the "curriculum." As my friend Jim Cathcart says, "You need to nurture their nature."

PRINCIPLE 3: SHOW THEM AND THEN LET THEM SHOW YOU. Parents make a mistake when they do not allow their children to demonstrate their developing skills. You can show a child how to play a musical instrument, but he won't become skilled at it until he plays it himself.

CHAPTER THIRTY-EIGHT

TRUE VALUE: THE REAL HARDWARE

*R**outine.*** Has it got you? The alarm goes off. Then you shower, get dressed, eat, make lunch, say good-bye, go to work, work, come home, eat, wind down, go to bed, and do it all again tomorrow. This may not be an accurate picture of your life as a parent and a spouse; however, we are all prone to fall into "the routine." While this is not entirely bad, it may foreshadow a silent destruction of the relationships that are most important to us. Wouldn't you agree that it is all too easy to take these relationships for granted?

If we are not adding value to the people we live with everyday, then it is possible they will begin to look for that value elsewhere—and that is the start of family disintegration. If you are not adding more to the family account than you are taking out, then it is time to do whatever it takes to close the gap.

Here are a few strategies for adding value to your family:

STRATEGY 1: KEEP YOUR PROMISES—PERIOD! Appointments with your loved ones are non-negotiable commitments. Keeping your promises is the most powerful form of leadership you can exercise as a parent.

STRATEGY 2: PLAN REGULARLY SCHEDULED FAMILY TIME. In my book, *The Power To Be Your Best!*, I explain how to master the art of time blocking. Here's my counsel: Put your family on your calendar *first*. If you don't, you will never spend the time with them that you could . . . or should.

STRATEGY 3: DEVELOP A FAMILY HOBBY. I still have great, indelible memories of being with my family while growing up: ski vacations, summers at the ranch, and ongoing outings and camping trips together. I'm now doing similar "family hobbies" with my own family.

STRATEGY 4: BE CONSISTENT; DON'T CRAM. You cannot make up for *not* adding value by suddenly dumping a whole bunch of it on the ones you love.

STRATEGY 5: DON'T KEEP SCORE. Adding value is not a game. Give your *whole* self—100 percent!

STRATEGY 6: SHOW AND TELL . . . YOUR LOVE. Do not give your family "half a loaf" by only *telling* them that you love them. You must tell *and show it* for maximum impact.

CHAPTER THIRTY-NINE

BIG BOYS DON'T CRY

Most of us know the myth: "Big boys don't cry." But the reality is: Big people not only cry, but *they need to cry.* That's because there is much to cry about: sickness, financial hardships, the death of a loved one, school children who die at the hands of classmates, boys and girls—here and abroad—who suffer and die from disease and malnutrition. To hold back your tears is to deny your humanity, and it prevents your family from seeing the real person you are. It is generally tougher for us males to express our emotions than it is for women. So let's focus on some concrete steps that men can take to help close this gap.

You may have seen it on television. It was one of the greatest golfing events of all time: the 1997 Masters. He was the first Asian-African American and the youngest player ever to win the event. Remarkably, he also won it with the lowest score ever. When Tiger Woods joined his dad on the eighteenth green, they hugged . . . and they cried.

The year was 1996, and I was with fifty-five thousand other men, listening to John Maxwell describe full-time dads as hot, warm, or cold. He asked us to reach deep within our souls to determine which of those we wanted to be. It was an emotional moment for me. Weeks later, I was watching the video of that presentation. I sat in amazement as the screen filled with the face of a man, his eyes closed, tears streaming down his face. That man was me!

Almost one year ago, my wife's mother passed away after nine years of battling cancer. I remember the first time I saw Lynn, her husband, after he lost his wife. We were in Michigan, and he and I were talking about Wilma. We hugged, and I could tell he wanted to cry. I squeezed him and said, "Go ahead, Lynn; it's okay." And he wept.

My mind often goes to the shortest verse in the Bible: John 11:35. It simply says, *"Jesus wept."*

In victory or loss, pain or joy, hurt or freedom, it is okay for men to cry. You may already know this, but please read on for the benefit of you and your sons.

There are three profound benefits to crying.

BENEFIT 1: THE ANCHORING OF JOY. You see it all the time. A sports team has a momentous victory, an individual athlete sets a world record, an everyday Jane or Joe does something no one thought possible. The thrill of victory hits us at our deepest emotional level. When this happens, it's okay to cry. To feel such high emotion—and to express it with tears—will imprint that event on your mind for the rest of your life.

BENEFIT 2: THE RELEASE OF GRIEF. On the other side of victory is loss. Whether it is a human or nonhuman event, pent-up grief is seldom healthy. Dry tear ducts lead to even deeper pain. Give yourself permission to cry. Express the pain you are feeling.

BENEFIT 3: INTIMACY WITH GOD. "Our God is an awesome God," the song says. If you are on track in your pursuit of spiritual abundance, then you surely have felt the presence of God in your life. As you now witness the Creator guiding your steps, stand in awe of His power. If His Spirit moves you cry, then cry. It will bring you even closer to Him.

*Tears are
God's gift to His
precious children.*
BARBARA JOHNSON

CHAPTER FORTY

THE FAMILY LIGHTHOUSE

Two battleships assigned to a training squadron had been at sea on maneuvers in heavy weather for several days. The visibility was poor with patchy fog, so the captain remained on the bridge, keeping an eye on all activities. . . . [when] the lookout . . . reported, "Light, bearing on the starboard bow" . . .

The captain said, "Send, I'm a captain, change course 20 degrees!"

"I'm a seaman second class," came the reply. "You had better change course 20 degrees."

By that time the captain was furious. He spat out, "Send, I'm a battleship. Change course 20 degrees."

Back came the flashing light, "I'm a lighthouse."

Is your family on a collision course with disaster? Or are you their lighthouse, determining their course and future as a family? If not, it's time to close the gap.

Most families haven't defined themselves. They haven't answered the important questions: *What is our purpose? What do we value? Where do we want to go individually and as a family? What short-term goals and activities will help us get there?* But parents must be the lighthouses of the family—a bright and sure mechanism that keeps everyone on the right course. When the parents' individual values are integrated with those of their family, all members will begin to work together for common purposes and goals. The following steps will help you guide your family.

- **Set up a summit meeting with your spouse.** During this time, both parents must address the questions cited above.

- **Set up a summit meeting with your children.** Share with them the findings of the summit with your spouse. Ask them to help you understand some of their own values and goals. Together, formulate these thoughts into a short working document.

- **Create the document.** At the top should be the *purpose of the family.* It should include areas of importance, such as spiritual, financial, physical, relational, and vocational. Then, for each area, write brief "job" descriptions (goals and related activities) for each family member.

- **Calendar the activities.** Put specific activities that relate to the family creed on the family calendar. Review your calendar at a weekly "team meeting."

PERSONAL
MASTERY

Try not to
become a person of
success but rather
a person of value.

ALBERT EINSTEIN

CHAPTER FORTY-ONE

NO COMPASS, NO MAP

F rom point A to point B, birth to death. It's an important journey, one that many people take without the proper guides. After all, you would not take an automobile trip across the country without referring to a road map. You would not trek the outback of Australia—or climb the rugged Sierra Nevada mountains in California—without a compass. Yet many of us live our lives without a compass or map, never giving a moment's thought about how we want our lives to look. If you are freewheeling your way through life with little or no direction, you are probably missing some of the greatest sights of all. Let's close this gap.

Most people are so busy making a living that they forget to design a life. They are simply taking life as it comes, making decisions as they go, rather than moving with confidence.

Henry David Thoreau said, "If one advances confidently in the direction of his dreams and endeavors to live the life which he has imagined, he will meet with success unexpected in common hours."

Catch the key words and phrases: *Advance confidently! Dreams! Imagine! Endeavor! Success!* Here are the four key steps to help you design your life:

STEP 1: DETERMINE YOUR "ACCOUNTS." Accounts are those areas of your life that you value most. These accounts, like the ones at the bank, require your attention and focus. The five most common life-accounts are spiritual, physical, financial, relational, and vocational.

STEP 2: DETERMINE YOUR VISION FOR EACH ACCOUNT. For each account, ask yourself, *In the next five, ten, or even fifteen years, what do I want this account to look like?*

STEP 3: DETERMINE YOUR ACTIONS IN EACH ACCOUNT. You will inevitably find gaps in each account. What actions will you take to close them?

STEP 4: SCHEDULE THE ACTIONS. The only way to advance confidently in the direction of your dreams is to act! You must turn new behaviors into solid habits that will last a lifetime. This is your map. Follow it!

CHAPTER FORTY-TWO

NOW YOU SEE ME; NOW YOU DON'T?

Personal mastery is most accurately defined as *alignment*. It is the process of making your activities consistent with your personal standards. If want to maintain a healthy weight, then your activities will include managed workouts and food consumption programs. If you desire intimacy with God, then your schedule will include studying the Scriptures, praying, and enjoying fellowship with others who share your beliefs. If you want to establish a vital marriage and family, then you will make time for dating your spouse, spending time with your children, and staying involved with your loved ones. However, for most people, there is a disparity between who they want to be on the inside and what their behavior reflects on the outside. If you are struggling with this inconsistency, then it is time to be authentic and close the gap.

"For what I am doing, I do not understand. For *what I will to do, that I do not practice; but what I hate, that I do."* ROMANS 7:15

Our beliefs set up certain principles that govern both what we do and who we are. When these are inconsistent, we experience conflict. At that moment, authenticity is an absolute requirement for growth. Simple willpower will not be enough to correct the problem; we must take ownership of our lives and begin to understand that our results will change only when we change our beliefs.

Mastery is a journey—a lifetime of striving for excellence. In pursuing personal mastery, here are two laws I have found to be true:

LAW 1: IF THE RESULTS OF YOUR BEHAVIOR DO NOT MEET YOUR NEEDS, THEN YOU MUST CHANGE YOUR BELIEFS. While I was addicted to cocaine, my belief was "It's cool." I quit using the substance when my belief changed to "This could kill me." My new behavior has been consistent with my belief for more than thirteen years.

LAW 2: REPETITION IS THE KEY TO SUSTAINED GROWTH. It is easier to close the gaps in your life when you repeat your new found actions. Then your confidence and self-worth will rise dramatically.

Become authentic! Identify your negative actions. Then change your beliefs.

CHAPTER FORTY-THREE

GIVING UP'S THE EASY PART

A life of excellence is not for everyone. In fact, it is not for most people. Many are only looking for a shortcut or a quick fix. Their life is a start-stop ritual, a forward-backward routine of mediocrity; their hallmark signature is *I quit!* These same people give up on God, on their bodies, on their relationships, and on their jobs—they give up on the disciplines required for a life of excellence.

I have a hunch that if you are still reading this book, then you are NOT one of these people. But do you know how to persevere with the passion and commitment that are characteristic of a winner? If not, then let's close the gap.

Life is a race that demands what every race requires—commitment. A commitment to run to the finish, overcoming seemingly insurmountable obstacles.

My friend Ted Engstrom, president emeritus of World Vision, once heard this amazing story from Art Linkletter:

"Last year she placed third . . . in the Iowa girls' state diving championships. . . . Now at the University of Florida, she's . . . earned the number-two position on the varsity diving team, and she's aiming for the national finals. Wendy is carrying a full academic load . . . and is an accomplished water-skier. But perhaps the most remarkable thing about Wendy Stoker is her typing. She bangs out forty-five words per minute . . . with her toes. . . . Wendy was born without arms."

How did Wendy do it? She quit feeling sorry for herself. She believed she had potential, and she acted. That is the commitment of a champion.

What is standing in the way of your success? Here are some thoughts on how to commit to a life of distinction:

• Nurture a passion for excellence. Do not accept mediocrity. Excellence is found in the heart, not the head.

• Develop a teachable spirit. Hunger for knowledge. Learn new skills.

• Exchange short-term pain for long-term gain. Excellence is reserved for those who understand that there are no shortcuts.

CHAPTER FORTY-FOUR

THE MYTH OF "MORE"

People say they want balance. Then they find themselves asking troubling questions, such as *I am wealthy, but why don't I feel happier? I am successful, but why don't I feel more satisfied?* and *I am busy, but why do I spend so much time on things that seem unimportant?*

The apostle Paul said, ". . . I have learned in whatever state I am, to be content: I know how to be abased, and I know how to abound. Everywhere and in all things I have learned both to be full and to be hungry" (Phil. 4:11–12). If you once thought that a newer car, a larger home, a bulging portfolio, or even a new spouse would bring you lasting contentment—but you came up short—then you know it is time to close the gap.

How much is "enough"? According to research conducted by *Fast Company* magazine, there is no such thing as enough—the more people have, the more they want. The study found that people with higher incomes (those making more than $100,000 per year) were "more likely . . . to view expensive cars, bigger houses, and dinners at fancy restaurants as their just desserts." At the other end of the financial spectrum, lower-income respondents (those making less than $40,000 per year) "agreed that learning to live on less money, and stuff, is an important factor in achieving balance in their lives." Whether your income is high or low, I believe that the true pathway to a life of riches is found in the thought processes of those respondents with lower incomes.

Contentment is a learned behavior. It does not happen when you have enough "stuff." There is nothing wrong with having goals, being financially responsible, or wanting a nice car and a comfortable home for your family. However, if you feel that these things will give you "ultimate contentment," you'll find that they will ever be enough.

Balance is something that happens over time. It is not something you suddenly enjoy when life slows down. Life will slow down when *you decide* to settle it down. Balance is a design matter. It comes down to choice.

CHAPTER FORTY-FIVE

WOE IS ME

The world in which we live is much like the clay on a potter's wheel. It turns endlessly, and what we do as it makes its revolutions is the difference between mastery and misery, between creating a masterpiece and presiding over a catastrophe.

Unfortunately, pessimism is everywhere. It is in the home, in the workplace, on the playing field, and even in the church. Why? What makes people so negative? Even if your attitude is severely tested, how does being negative help move you closer to the land of your dreams? Here is the bottom line: *More than anything else, your attitude determines your ultimate success.* If you would like to turn your "woe is me" into "joy is me," here are some proven principles to help you close the gap.

"Finish every day and be done with it. . . .
Some blunders and absurdities no doubt crept in; forget them as
fast as you can. Tomorrow is a new day." RALPH WALDO EMERSON

There is only one way to live a life of fulfillment and joy:
You must develop and maintain a healthy, positive attitude.
With this attitude, you will live longer, enjoy more success,
and develop more meaningful relationships. Most importantly,
you will enjoy this incredible journey called "life."

Do you want to be known as a person who approaches life
with a positive attitude? If so, follow these steps:

- Believe that God has a plan for your life.
- Believe in yourself and the role that you play in that plan.
- Look at adversity as God's way of continuing to perfect you.
- See your life as the masterpiece it is.
- Be solution-focused, not problem-based.
- Get into the habit of loving people.
- Be a giver, not a taker.
- Be fully responsible.
- Learn from your every mistake.

Life becomes synergistic when you become positive.
Suddenly you begin to attract positive circumstances and positive
people into your life—especially when you surround yourself
with a spirit of excellence. Remember that it is not what happens
to you that counts; *it's what you do about what happens to you.*

CLOSING YOUR GAPS IS UP TO YOU

One of my clients made an enormous impact on me when he showed me a poem that he shared with his kids early in their lives. To this day, he and his wife and children live each exciting day with the positive message it contains. I now share it with you.

If you think you are beaten, you are.

If you think you dare not, you don't.

If you like to win, but you think you can't,

It is almost certain you won't.

If you think you'll lose, you're lost.

For out of the world we find,

Success begins with a person's will—

It's all in the state of mind.

If you think you're outclassed, you are.

You've got to think high to rise,

You've got to be sure of yourself before

You can ever win the prize.

Life's battles don't always go

To the stronger woman or man,

But sooner or later the one who wins . . .

Is the one WHO THINKS HE CAN!

I wish you total and complete happiness and fulfillment as you close the gaps in your life. May you always . . . be your best!

Todd Duncan

ACKNOWLEDGEMENTS

Grateful acknowledgement is made to the following:

Carnegie Council on Adolescent Development. 1995. *Great Transitions: Preparing Adolescents for a New Century.* Carnegie Corporation: New York.

Habib, Barry. President of Certified Mortgage Associates. (732) 946-2233

Harkavy, Daniel. CEO and Coach of Building Champions. (503) 699-4141. www.buildingchampions.com

Salsbury, Glenna. Professional speaker and author. Paradise Valley, Arizona. (480) 483-7732. www.glennasalsbury.com

Swindoll, Charles. 1996. *Intimacy with the Almighty.* Word Publishing: Nashville, Tennessee.

Vance, Mike. Kitchen of the Mind™ concept.

Story on page 133 reprinted with permission from Art Linkletter. 1983. Single cassette recording. Nightingale-Conant Corporation: Chicago.

Story on page 124 reprinted from *Proceedings* with permission. Copyright © 1987 United States Naval Institute. Author: Frank Koch.

Research on page 135 reprinted from the July 1999 issue of *Fast Company* magazine. All rights reserved. To subscribe, please call (800) 688-1545.